Underwater De...

by H... ...
Illustrated by Rose Wilkinson

Contents

Meet Pearl!	2
Our blue planet	3
Coral reefs	9
Polar seas	13
Mysteries of the deep	17
Plants and seaweed	21
Coasts	23
Find out more about Dr Pearl Mariana	28
Glossary	31
Index	32

OXFORD UNIVERSITY PRESS

Meet Pearl!

"Every day, I learn more about our wonderful seas and oceans, and how we can protect them."

Pearl

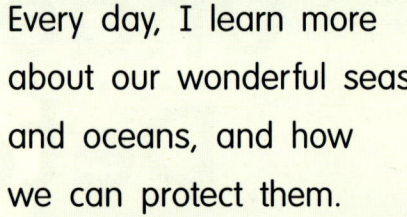

Pearl is a **marine** scientist. Marine scientists study animals and plants that live in the sea. This includes everything from huge whales swimming across oceans to tiny shrimps dashing around rock pools.

Pearl studies how marine creatures and plants live alongside each other.

Our blue planet

Pearl is travelling around the world's oceans because she is writing a book about marine science.

Before Pearl goes out on her boat, she fills a water bottle with water from the tap. This is because seawater is salty and we cannot drink it.

About 70% of the Earth's **surface** is covered by water, but most of that water is salty. The water we drink is called 'fresh water'. It mainly comes from rivers and lakes.

Today, I'm exploring the Caribbean Sea near my home.

There are five oceans on our planet.

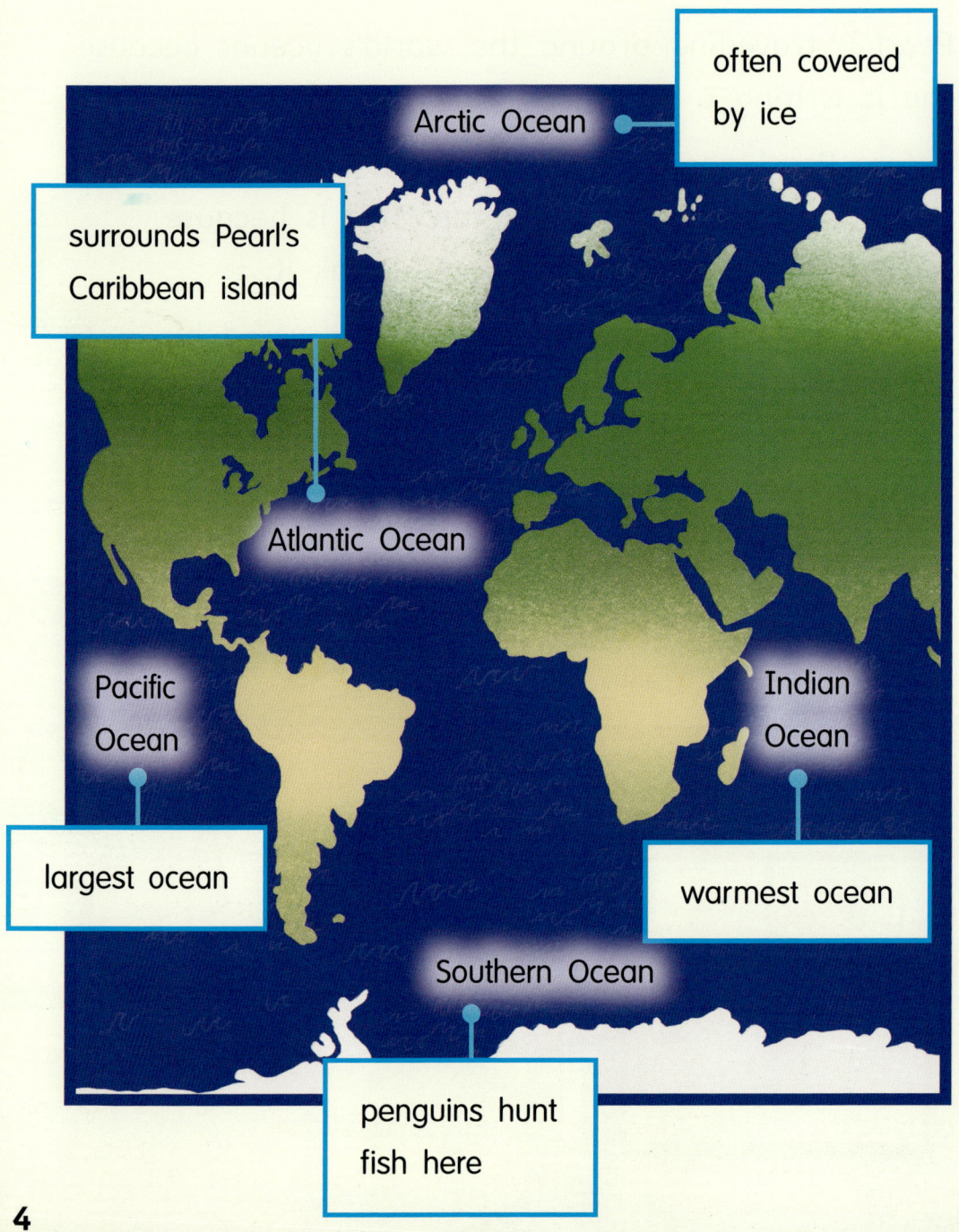

We cannot drink seawater, but we could not live on Earth without our oceans. That is why Pearl is so interested in them.

Six reasons the oceans are important:

1 Air

Our oceans make more than half the world's oxygen. Oxygen is an important part of the air we breathe.

2 Food

Our oceans provide us with food to eat, like **shellfish**, fish and seaweed.

My favourite food is grilled shrimp. Shrimp is a type of shellfish.

3 Weather

When the sun shines on the Earth, our oceans heat up. The oceans move this warm water around the world. This creates different weather such as rain and wind. If the oceans did not move the warm water around, the weather where you live would be very different. It could become hotter or cooler. It could become wetter or dryer. Our oceans help to keep the world's weather predictable.

4 Travel

We can travel around the world by boat, discovering new and interesting places. We can also move things from one part of the world to another in huge cargo ships. Many of the things you buy in the shops have travelled across the world by ship.

5 Fun

Our seas are great fun, too! You can go swimming, sailing, fishing, snorkelling and kayaking in the sea.

> **6 Wildlife**
>
> Our oceans are bursting with wildlife. Half of all life on Earth today lives in the oceans. Marine scientists think there are many creatures in the oceans that we have not even discovered yet.

Pearl is like an underwater detective searching for clues about our hidden world. She wants to understand the world's oceans better so we can protect and manage them.

Coral reefs

Some of the most colourful places where Pearl works are coral **reefs**. There are coral reefs all over the world. They can be found in shallow, clear and warm seas.

Pearl goes snorkelling in the Caribbean Sea near her home. She checks that the coral is healthy.

This coral reef looks healthy.

snorkel

fins

mask

the Great Barrier Reef

The largest and most famous coral reef is called the Great Barrier Reef. It is near the coast of Australia and is so big that it can be seen from space!

Living corals may look like a plant, or sometimes a rock, but they are actually lots of tiny animals living together. These groups of corals are called reefs. Reefs are home to many different plants, fish and animals.

Corals, sea anemones and **sponges** look like plants, but they are all animals.

- turtle
- puffer fish
- shark
- coral
- sea anemone
- sponge
- clownfish
- octopus

Pearl loves coral reefs because they are full of wildlife. However, they are under threat for many reasons:

- our oceans are becoming too warm
- the water is too dirty
- people can damage coral reefs when they go diving or use powerboats and jet skis
- too much fishing means there are fewer fish.

Pearl teaches tourists how to have fun around coral reefs without damaging them. She also gives advice on what type of fish it is OK to catch.

This coral reef is dying because the sea here is too warm and dirty.

Pearl is moving some of the coral to make a new reef in a cleaner and cooler part of the ocean. This takes time, but if it works people will be able to enjoy these beautiful reefs in the future.

Pearl is checking the coral on this frame. The coral will grow over time.

Polar seas

Now, Pearl has travelled somewhere very different from the warm, shallow seas of the Caribbean.

She is in Antarctica studying the Southern Ocean. Nobody lives here full-time because it is too cold. Pearl stays at a special research station with other scientists.

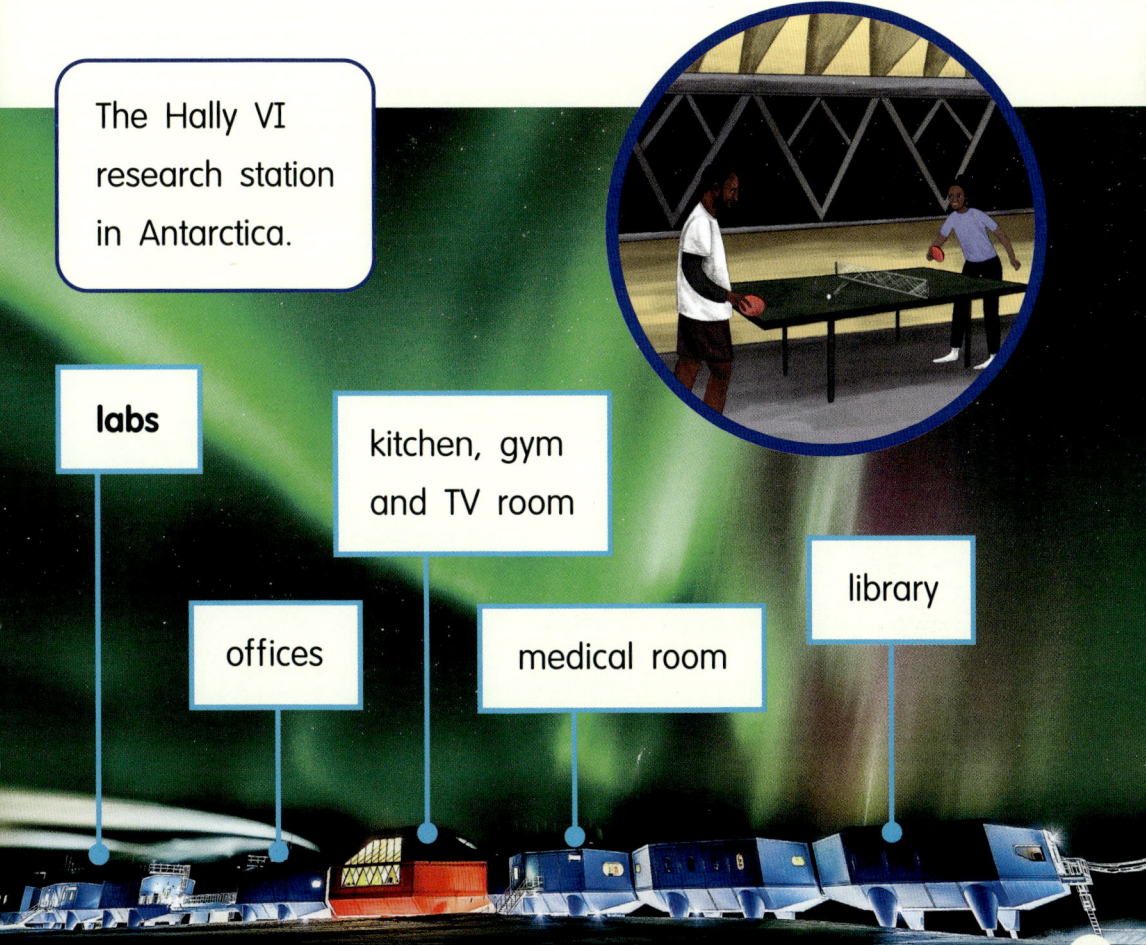

The Hally VI research station in Antarctica.

labs

kitchen, gym and TV room

library

offices

medical room

Pearl is researching how different animals **survive** in these freezing waters. She makes a hole in the sea ice and builds a hut over the hole. This helps protect it from the weather. Then she dives through the hole to record the animals she finds. She wears a special **dry suit** with a hood and gloves to keep her warm. She cannot stay in the freezing-cold water for long.

Penguins hunt krill, but they also eat squid and fish.

Krill are small, shrimp-like animals. Almost all ocean life depends on krill because so many fish, seals, birds and whales eat them.

While she is in Antarctica, Pearl sees emperor penguins. They are the largest penguins in the world. They cannot fly, but they are very good at diving!

Pearl also travels to the other side of the world – to the Arctic. Between December and May, most of the Arctic Ocean freezes over. Polar bears hunt for seals on the ice, and walruses breed there.

Our oceans are becoming warmer, which is making the polar ice melt. This makes it harder for animals to hunt and breed. Scientists record how much polar ice is melting every year. They are trying to find ways to help animals survive if the ice continues to melt.

Mysteries of the deep

It is difficult for Pearl to explore the polar oceans, but deep oceans are even more difficult to visit. We know more about the moon than we do about our deepest oceans! It is likely that there are all sorts of creatures in the deep that we have not discovered yet.

Pearl uses a research ship to explore deep parts of the Pacific Ocean for her book. The ship has labs, offices, bedrooms and even small submarines on board.

It is very dark in the deep oceans so some animals, like jellyfish, glow in the dark. Others, like the football fish, have a blue light over their heads which is a bit like a torch. Some fish have large eyes so they can see better. Others cannot see at all.

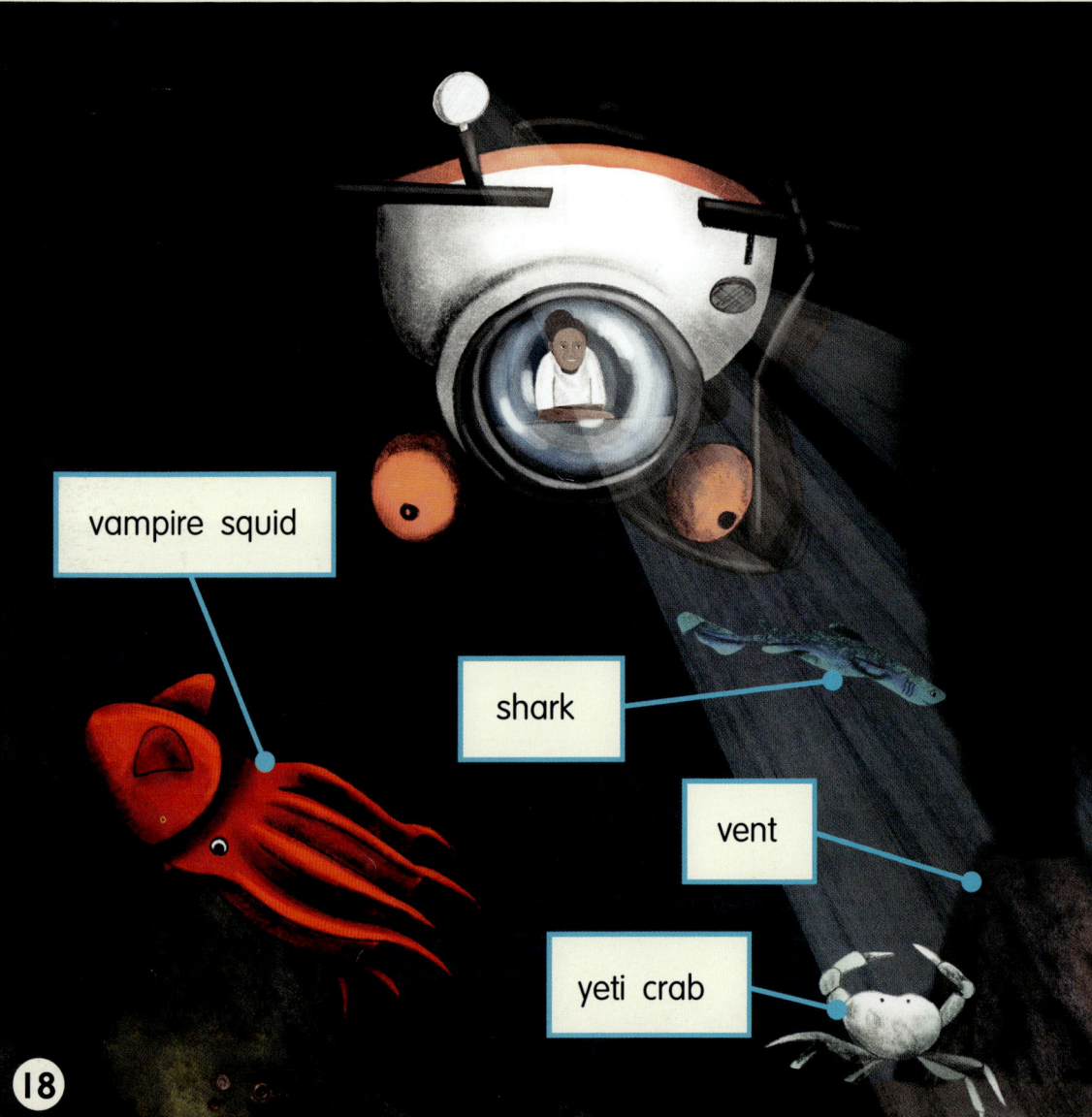

Marine scientists, like Pearl, are interested in deep oceans for many reasons. There may be metals we can dig up, new medicines to discover, new sources of food, and more. The deep oceans can also help us understand things like earthquakes better.

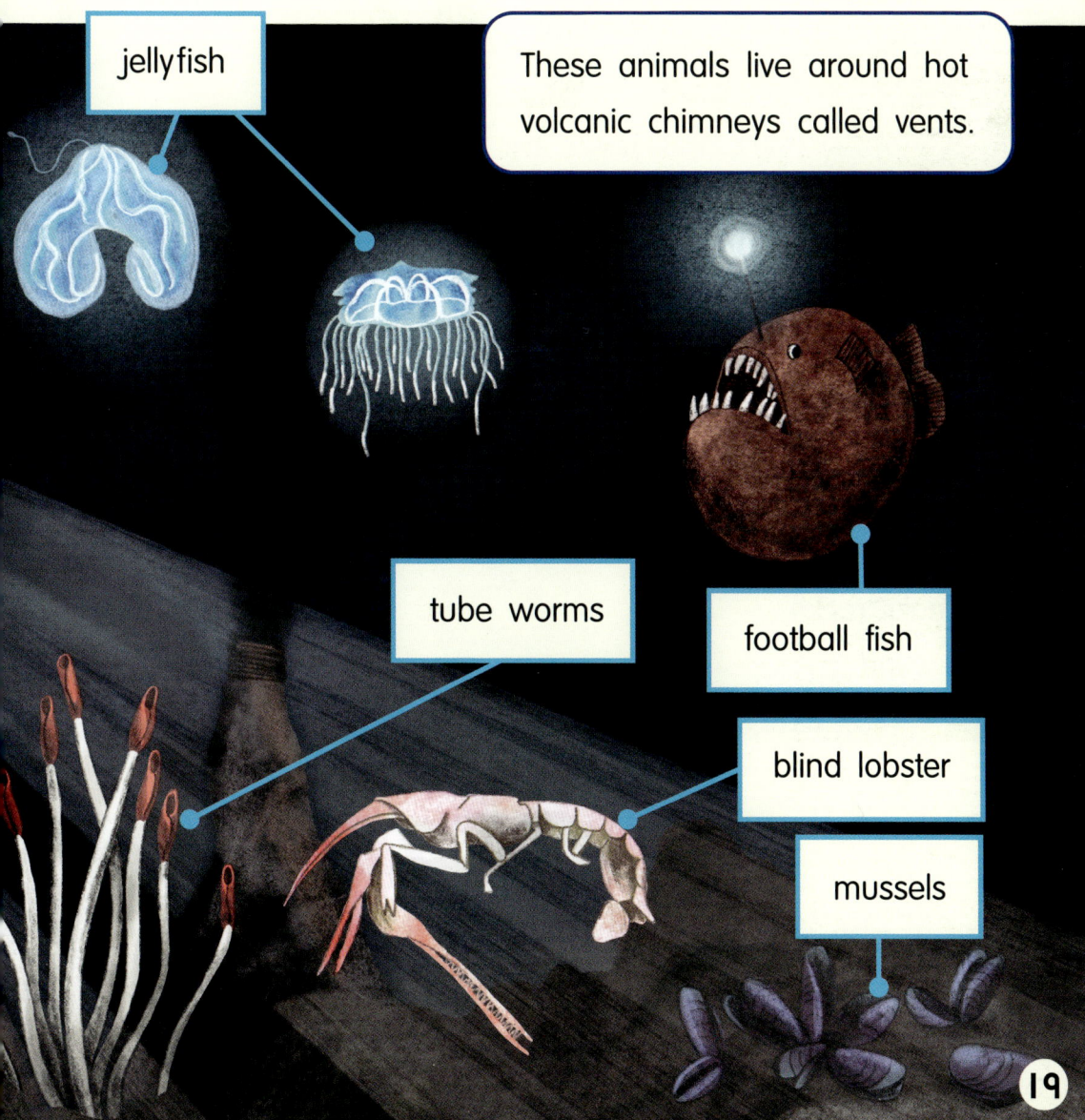

jellyfish

These animals live around hot volcanic chimneys called vents.

tube worms

football fish

blind lobster

mussels

Pearl cannot dive in very deep water because it is too cold and dark, and the water pressure is too dangerous. Instead, she uses an underwater robot.

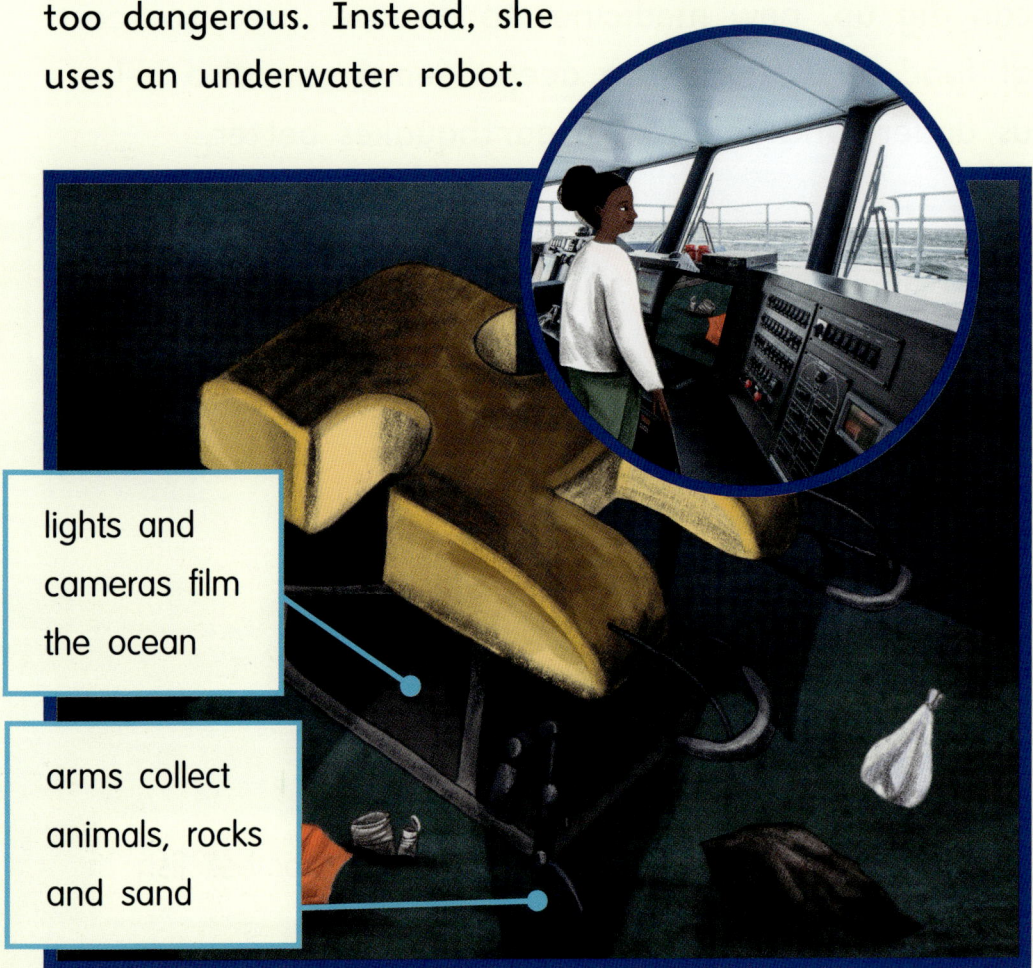

lights and cameras film the ocean

arms collect animals, rocks and sand

Pearl watches the robot's video in her office on the research ship. She sees many amazing creatures. Sadly, she often sees rubbish in the videos too, even in the deepest parts of our oceans.

Plants and seaweed

Pearl wants to write about new uses for marine plants and seaweed in her book. Without plants, the ocean's animals would not be able to survive.

Seagrass, kelp forests and mangrove trees grow in shallow water all over the world. They shelter large numbers of animals, especially during storms. Many fish lay their eggs among these plants to keep the eggs safe. When the baby fish grow bigger, they can head out to the open sea.

This kelp is growing around the coast of the UK.

Sea plants and seaweed are important for people, too. They clean the sea and put oxygen in the air. They also help protect the land from waves and storm damage.

Some seagrass meadows and mangrove forests around the world have been damaged by farming, building and fishing. For thousands of years, seagrass has been used to make furniture, roofs and even bandages.

heron

manatee

mangrove tree

seagrass

Pearl plants young seagrass to help this meadow in the UK regrow.

Coasts

Waves smash against rocky cliffs in the UK. Over time, this wears the cliffs down and changes their shape. Pearl is always careful to stay away from the edge. There is a steep drop down to the sea below.

cliffs

cave

bay

It's exciting to visit coral reefs and deep oceans, but I love the seaside, with its cliffs and beaches, too.

Clifftops are home to many different nesting birds, such as puffins and seagulls. They fly out to sea where they catch fish and sand eels to feed to their chicks.

Pearl records which birds she sees and how many there are, so we know which birds are doing well and which birds might need help.

If you have a dog, keep it on a lead. It might scare the birds away from their clifftop nests.

These puffins have sand eels in their beaks.

When the **tide** goes out, Pearl investigates rock pools on the beach. They are full of life. Sea anemones wave their tentacles to catch food. Crabs scuttle from one hiding place to another. Tiny shrimps dart about the seaweed. Barnacles and limpets cling onto the rocks.

You can use a cup to carefully catch creatures in a rock pool, but always put them back before you go home.

It is time for Pearl to go back home to the Caribbean.

On her local beach, turtles dig big holes in the sand and lay their eggs. They cover the eggs with sand and then head back into the ocean. Pearl puts a sign next to each nest so people do not disturb them.

When the baby turtles hatch, they must run into the sea. Some of them get a bit lost so Pearl helps them find their way.

Pearl organizes litter-picking on the beach. Sea creatures can get caught up in rubbish. Some animals, like turtles, mistake plastic bags for jellyfish and eat them. This makes them ill.

Pearl hopes her book will teach people how to protect our oceans and all the creatures that live in them. Whether we live by the sea or not, we all need to care for our oceans, just like Pearl.

Find out more about Dr Pearl Mariana

Q Why did you want to be a marine scientist?

A I loved the ocean as a little girl. Whenever we went to the coast on holiday, my parents couldn't keep me out of the water.  I was fascinated by what was in the ocean. It's a completely different world below the surface.

Q What is the best thing about your job?

A I travel all over the world, discovering amazing plants and animals. It's never boring.

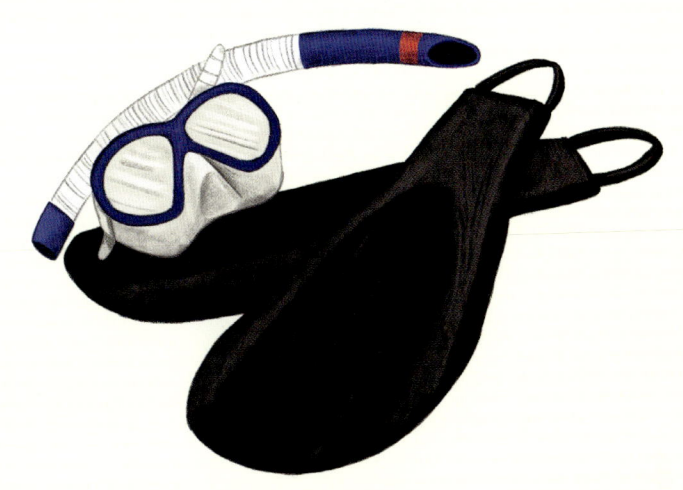

Q Do you work on or in the ocean all the time?

A No, I don't. For every hour I spend in the water, I spend about five hours in my office writing reports and researching.

Q What are you proudest of?

A I'm proudest of sharing all the things I've learned with other people, so we can all do our bit to protect our oceans.

Q What is your favourite sea creature?

A There are millions of amazing sea creatures so it's hard to pick one. I am very interested in corals. I like finding ways to help them survive.

Q Which ocean would you most like to explore?

A I would love to explore a protected coral reef in the Indian Ocean. It's teeming with marine life.

Q What tips would you give children who want to be marine scientists?

A Learn to swim. Start reading everything you can about the sea and what's in it. It's an amazing job!

Glossary

dry suit: a piece of clothing that keeps water out

labs: where scientists carry out tests

marine: to do with the sea

reefs: lines of rocks, coral or sand under the water

shellfish: sea creatures with a shell; for example crabs and oysters

sponges: sea creatures with light bodies full of holes

surface: the top layer of something

survive: to continue to live

tide: the regular rise and fall of the level of the sea

Index

Antarctica 13, 15

Arctic 4, 16

beach 23, 25, 26–27

Caribbean 3, 4, 9, 13, 26

coral 9, 10–11, 12, 23, 30

fish 4–5, 10–11, 14–15, 18–19, 21, 24

fishing 7, 11, 22

ice 4, 14, 16

jellyfish 18–19, 27

rubbish 20, 27

seaweed 5, 21, 22, 25

ship 7, 17, 20

shrimp 2, 5, 15, 25

snorkelling 7, 9

turtle 10, 26–27